2

THE OPEN MEDIA PAMPHLET SERIES

Media Control

The Spectacular Achievements of Propaganda

NOAM CHOMSKY

SEVEN STORIES PRESS / New York

A Seven Stories Press First Edition,
published in association with Open Media.

Open Media Pamphlet Series editors,
Greg Ruggiero and Stuart Sahulka.

Library of Congress Cataloging-in-Publication Data

Chomsky, Noam.
    Media control: the spectacular achievements of
propaganda / Noam Chomsky.
    p.   cm. —(The Open Media Pamphlet Series)
    ISBN 1-888363-49-5
    1. Propaganda. 2. Propaganda—United States. 3.
Mass media—Political aspects. 4. Mass media and
public opinion. I. Title. II. Series.
HM263.C447 1997
303.3'75—dc21   96-53580
                                         CIP

Book design by Cindy LaBreacht

9 8 7 6 5 4 3 2

The role of the media in contemporary politics forces us to ask what kind of a world and what kind of a society we want to live in, and in particular in what sense of democracy do we want this to be a democratic society? Let me begin by counter-posing two different conceptions of democracy. One conception of democracy has it that a democratic society is one in which the public has the means to participate in some meaningful way in the management of their own affairs and the means of information are open and free. If you look up democracy in the dictionary you'll get a definition something like that.

An alternative conception of democracy is that the public must be barred from managing of their own affairs and the means of information must be kept narrowly and rigidly controlled. That may sound like an odd conception of democracy, but it's important to understand that it is the prevailing conception. In fact, it has long been, not just in operation, but even in theory. There's a long history that goes back to the earliest modern democratic revolutions in seventeenth century England which largely expresses this point of view. I'm just going to keep to the modern period and say a few words about how that notion of democracy develops and why and how the problem of media and disinformation enters within that context.

EARLY HISTORY OF PROPAGANDA

Let's begin with the first modern government propaganda operation. That was under the Woodrow Wilson Administration. Woodrow Wilson was elected President in 1916 on the platform "Peace Without Victory." That was right in the middle of the World War I. The population was extremely pacifistic and saw no reason to become involved in a European war. The Wilson administration was actually committed to war and had to do something about it. They established a government propaganda commission, called the Creel Commission, which succeeded, within six months, in turning a pacifist population into a hysterical, war–mongering population which wanted to destroy everything German, tear the Germans limb from limb, go to war and save the world. That was a major achievement, and it led to a further achievement. Right at that time and after the war the same techniques were used to whip up a hysterical Red Scare, as it was called, which succeeded pretty much in destroying unions and eliminating such dangerous problems as freedom of the press and freedom of political thought. There was very strong support from the media, from the business establishment, which in fact organized, pushed much of this work, and it was, in general, a great success.

Among those who participated actively and enthusiastically in Wilson's war were the progressive intellectuals, people of the John Dewey circle, who took great pride, as you can see from their own writings at the time, in having shown that what they called the "more intelligent members of the community," namely, themselves, were able to drive a reluctant population into a war by terrifying them and eliciting jingoist fanaticism. The means that were used were extensive. For example, there was a good deal of fabrication of atrocities by the Huns, Belgian babies with their arms torn off, all sorts of awful things that you still read in history books. Much of it was invented by the British propaganda ministry, whose own commitment at the time, as they put it in their secret deliberations, was "to direct the thought of most of the world." But more crucially they wanted to control the thought of the more intelligent members of the community in the United States, who would then disseminate the propaganda that they were concocting and convert the pacifistic country to wartime hysteria. That worked. It worked very well. And it taught a lesson: State propaganda, when supported by the educated classes and when no deviation is permitted from it, can have a big effect. It was a lesson learned by Hitler and many others, and it has been pursued to this day.

SPECTATOR DEMOCRACY

Another group that was impressed by these successes was liberal democratic theorists and leading media figures, like, for example, Walter Lippmann, who was the dean of American journalists, a major foreign and domestic policy critic and also a major theorist of liberal democracy. If you take a look at his collected essays, you'll see that they're subtitled something like "A Progressive Theory of Liberal Democratic Thought." Lippmann was involved in these propaganda commissions and recognized their achievements. He argued that what he called a "revolution in the art of democracy," could be used to "manufacture consent, " that is, to bring about agreement on the part of the public for things that they didn't want by the new techniques of propaganda. He also thought that this was a good idea, in fact, necessary. It was necessary because, as he put it, "the common interests elude public opinion entirely" and can only be understood and managed by a "specialized class "of "responsible men" who are smart enough to figure things out. This theory asserts that only a small elite, the intellectual community that the Deweyites were talking about, can understand the common interests, what all of us care about, and that these things "elude the general public." This is a view that goes back hundreds of years. It's also a typical Leninist view. In fact, it has very close resemblance to the Leninist conception that a vanguard of revolutionary intellectuals take state power, using popular revolutions as the force that brings them to state power, and then drive the stupid masses toward a future that they're too dumb and incompetent to envision for themselves. The liberal democratic theory and Marxism–Leninism are very close in their common ideological assumptions. I think that's one reason why people have found it so easy over the years to drift from one position to another without any particular sense of change. It's just a matter of assessing where power is. Maybe there will be a popular revolution, and that will put us into state power; or maybe there won't be, in which case we'll just work for the people with real power: the business community. But we'll do the same thing. We'll drive the stupid masses toward a world that they're too dumb to understand for themselves.

Lippmann backed this up by a pretty elaborated theory of progressive democracy. He argued that in a properly functioning democracy there are classes of citizens. There is first of all the class of citizens who have to take some active role in running general affairs. That's the specialized class. They are the people who analyze, execute, make decisions, and run things in the political, economic, and ideological systems. That's a small percentage of the population. Naturally, anyone who puts these ideas forth is always part of that small group, and they're talking about what to do about *those others*. Those others, who are out of the small group, the big majority of the population, they are what Lippmann called "the bewildered herd." We have to protect ourselves from "the trampling and roar of a bewildered herd". Now there are two "functions" in a democracy: The specialized class, the responsible men, carry out the executive function, which means they do the thinking and planning and understand the common interests. Then, there is the bewildered herd, and they have a function in democracy too. Their function in a democracy, he said, is to be "spectators," not participants in action. But they have more of a function than that, because it's a

NOAM CHOMSKY

democracy. Occasionally they are allowed to lend their weight to one or another member of the specialized class. In other words, they're allowed to say, "We want you to be our leader" or "We want *you* to be our leader." That's because it's a democracy and not a totalitarian state. That's called an election. But once they've lent their weight to one or another member of the specialized class they're supposed to sink back and become spectators of action, but not participants. That's in a properly functioning democracy.

And there's a logic behind it. There's even a kind of compelling moral principle behind it. The compelling moral principle is that the mass of the public are just too stupid to be able to understand things. If they try to participate in managing their own affairs, they're just going to cause trouble. Therefore, it would be immoral and improper to permit them to do this. We have to tame the bewildered herd, not allow the bewildered herd to rage and trample and destroy things. It's pretty much the same logic that says that it would be improper to let a three-year-old run across the street. You don't give a three-year-old that kind of freedom because the three-year-old doesn't know how to handle that freedom.

Correspondingly, you don't allow the bewildered herd to become participants in action. They'll just cause trouble.

So we need something to tame the bewildered herd, and that something is this new revolution in the art of democracy: the manufacture of consent. The media, the schools, and popular culture have to be divided. For the political class and the decision makers they have to provide them some tolerable sense of reality, although they also have to instill the proper beliefs. Just remember, there is an unstated premise here. The unstated premise —and even the responsible men have to disguise this from themselves—has to do with the question of how they get into the position where they have the authority to make decisions. The way they do that, of course, is by serving people with *real* power. The people with real power are the ones who own the society, which is a pretty narrow group. If the specialized class can come along and say, I can serve your interests, then they'll be part of the executive group. You've got to keep that quiet. That means they have to have instilled in them the beliefs and doctrines that will serve the interests of private power. Unless they can master that skill, they're not part of the spe-

NOAM CHOMSKY

cialized class. So we have one kind of educational system directed to the responsible men, the specialized class. They have to be deeply indoctrinated in the values and interests of private power and the state-corporate nexus that represents it. If they can achieve that, then they can be part of the specialized class. The rest of the bewildered herd basically just have to be distracted. Turn their attention to something else. Keep them out of trouble. Make sure that they remain at most spectators of action, occasionally lending their weight to one or another of the real leaders, who they may select among.

This point of view has been developed by lots of other people. In fact, it's pretty conventional. For example, the leading theologian and foreign policy critic Reinhold Niebuhr, sometimes called "the theologian of the establishment," the guru of George Kennan and the Kennedy intellectuals, put it that rationality is a very narrowly restricted skill. Only a small number of people have it. Most people are guided by just emotion and impulse. Those of us who have rationality have to create "necessary illusions" and emotionally potent "oversimpli-fications" to keep the naïve simpletons more or less on course. This became a substantial part of contemporary political science. In the 1920s and early 1930s, Harold Lasswell, the founder of the modern field of communications and one of the leading American political scientists, explained that we should not succumb to "democratic dogmatisms about men being the best judges of their own interests." Because they're not. We're the best judges of the public interests. Therefore, just out of ordinary morality, we have to make sure that they don't have an opportunity to act on the basis of their misjudgments. In what is nowadays called a totalitarian state, or a military state, it's easy. You just hold a bludgeon over their heads, and if they get out of line you smash them over the head. But as society has become more free and democratic, you lose that capacity. Therefore you have to turn to the techniques of propaganda. The logic is clear. Propaganda is to a democracy what the bludgeon is to a totalitarian state. That's wise and good because, again, the common interests elude the bewildered herd. They can't figure them out.

NOAM CHOMSKY

PUBLIC RELATIONS

The United States pioneered the public relations industry. Its commitment was "to control the public mind," as its leaders put it. They learned a lot from the successes of the Creel Commission and the successes in creating the Red Scare and its aftermath. The public relations industry underwent a huge expansion at that time. It succeeded for some time in creating almost total subordination of the public to business rule through the 1920s. This was so extreme that Congressional committees began to investigate it as we moved into the 1930s. That's where a lot of our information about it comes from.

Public relations is a huge industry. They're spending by now something on the order of a billion dollars a year. All along its commitment was to *controlling the public mind*. In the 1930s, big problems arose again, as they had during the First World War. There was a huge depression and substantial labor organizing. In fact, in 1935 labor won its first major legislative victory, namely, the right to organize, with the Wagner Act. That raised two serious problems. For one thing, democracy was misfunctioning. The bewildered herd was actually winning legislative victories, and it's not supposed to work that way. The other problem was that it was becoming possible for people to organize. People have to be atomized and segregated and alone. They're not supposed to organize, because then they might be something beyond spectators of action. They might actually be participants if many people with limited resources could get together to enter the political arena. That's really threatening. A major response was taken on the part of business to ensure that this would be the last legislative victory for labor and that it would be the beginning of the end of this democratic deviation of popular organization. It worked. That was the last legislative victory for labor. From that point on—although the number of people in the unions increased for a while during the World War II, after which it started dropping—the capacity to act through the unions began to steadily drop. It wasn't by accident. We're now talking about the business community, which spends lots and lots of money, attention, and thought into how to deal with these problems through the public relations industry and other organizations, like the

National Association of Manufacturers and the Business Roundtable, and so on. They immediately set to work to try to find a way to counter these democratic deviations.

The first trial was one year later, in 1937. There was a major strike, the Steel strike in western Pennsylvania at Johnstown. Business tried out a new technique of labor destruction, which worked very well. Not through goon squads and breaking knees. That wasn't working very well any more, but through the more subtle and effective means of propaganda. The idea was to figure out ways to turn the public against the strikers, to present the strikers as disruptive, harmful to the public and against the common interests. The common interests are those of "us," the businessman, the worker, the housewife. That's all "us." We want to be together and have things like harmony and Americanism and working together. Then there's those bad strikers out there who are disruptive and causing trouble and breaking harmony and violating Americanism. We've got to stop them so we can all live together. The corporate executive and the guy who cleans the floors all have the same interests. We can all work together and work for Americanism in harmony, liking each other.

That was essentially the message. A huge amount of effort was put into presenting it. This is, after all, the business community, so they control the media and have massive resources. And it worked, very effectively. It was later called the "Mohawk Valley formula" and applied over and over again to break strikes. They were called "scientific methods of strike-breaking," and worked very effectively by mobilizing community opinion in favor of vapid, empty concepts like Americanism. Who can be against that? Or harmony. Who can be against that? Or, as in the Persian Gulf War, "Support our troops." Who can be against that? Or yellow ribbons. Who can be against that? Anything that's totally vacuous.

In fact, what does it mean if somebody asks you, Do you support the people in Iowa? Can you say, Yes, I support them, or No, I don't support them? It's not even a question. It doesn't mean anything. That's the point. The point of public relations slogans like "Support our troops" is that they don't mean anything. They mean as much as whether you support the people in Iowa. Of course, there was an issue. The issue was, Do you support our policy? But you don't want people to think about that issue. That's the whole point of good propaganda.

NOAM CHOMSKY

You want to create a slogan that nobody's going to be against, and everybody's going to be for. Nobody knows what it means, because it doesn't mean anything. Its crucial value is that it diverts your attention from a question that *does* mean something: Do you support our policy? That's the one you're not allowed to talk about. So you have people arguing about support for the troops? "Of course I don't *not* support them." Then you've won. That's like Americanism and harmony. We're all together, empty slogans, let's join in, let's make sure we don't have these bad people around to disrupt our harmony with their talk about class struggle, rights and that sort of business.

That's all very effective. It runs right up to today. And of course it is carefully thought out. The people in the public relations industry aren't there for the fun of it. They're doing work. They're trying to instill the right values. In fact, they have a conception of what democracy ought to be: It ought to be a system in which the specialized class is trained to work in the service of the masters, the people who own the society. The rest of the population ought to be deprived of any form of organization, because organization just causes trouble.

They ought to be sitting alone in front of the TV and having drilled into their heads the message, which says, the only value in life is to have more commodities or live like that rich middle class family you're watching and to have nice values like harmony and Americanism. That's all there is in life. You may think in your own head that there's got to be something more in life than this, but since you're watching the tube alone you assume, I must be crazy, because that's all that's going on over there. And since there is no organization permitted—that's absolutely crucial—you never have a way of finding out whether you are crazy, and you just assume it, because it's the natural thing to assume.

So that's the ideal. Great efforts are made in trying to achieve that ideal. Obviously, there is a certain conception behind it. The conception of democracy is the one that I mentioned. The bewildered herd is a problem. We've got to prevent their roar and trampling. We've got to distract them. They should be watching the Superbowl or sitcoms or violent movies. Every once in a while you call on them to chant meaningless slogans like "Support our troops." You've got to keep them pretty scared, because unless they're properly scared and frightened of all kinds of devils that are going to destroy them from outside or inside or somewhere, they may start to think, which is very dangerous, because they're not competent to think. Therefore it's important to distract them and marginalize them.

That's one conception of democracy. In fact, going back to the business community, the last legal victory for labor really was 1935, the Wagner Act. After the war came, the unions declined as did a very rich working class culture that was associated with the unions. That was destroyed. We moved to a business–run society at a remarkable level. This is the only state-capitalist industrial society which doesn't have even the normal social contract that you find in comparable societies. Outside of South Africa, I guess, this is the only industrial society that doesn't have national health care. There's no general commitment to even minimal standards of survival for the parts of the population who can't follow those rules and gain things for themselves individually. Unions are virtually nonexistent. Other forms of popular structure are virtually nonexistent. There are no political parties or organizations. It's a long way toward the ideal, at least structurally. The media are a corporate monopoly.

They have the same point of view. The two parties are two factions of the business party. Most of the population doesn't even bother voting because it looks meaningless. They're marginalized and properly distracted. At least that's the goal. The leading figure in the public relations industry, Edward Bernays, actually came out of the Creel Commission. He was part of it, learned his lessons there and went on to develop what he called the "engineering of consent," which he described as "the essence of democracy." The people who are able to engineer consent are the ones who have the resources and the power to do it—the business community—and that's who you work for.

ENGINEERING OPINION

It is also necessary to whip up the population in support of foreign adventures. Usually the population is pacifist, just like they were during the First World War. The public sees no reason to get involved in foreign adventures, killing, and torture. So you *have* to whip them up. And to whip them up you have to frighten them. Bernays himself had an important achievement in this respect. He was the person who ran the public relations campaign for the United Fruit Company in 1954, when the United States moved in to overthrow the capitalist-democratic government of Guatemala and installed a murderous death-squad society, which remains that way to the present day with constant infusions of U.S. aid to prevent in more than empty form democratic deviations. It's necessary to constantly ram through domestic programs which the public is opposed to, because there is no reason for the public to be in favor of domestic programs that are harmful to them. *This*, too, takes extensive propaganda. We've seen a lot of this in the last ten years. The Reagan programs were overwhelmingly unpopular. Voters in the 1984 "Reagan landslide," by about three to two, hoped that his policies would not be enacted. If you take particular programs, like armaments, cutting back on social spending, etc., almost every one of them was overwhelmingly opposed by the public. But as long as people are marginalized and distracted and have no way to organize or articulate their sentiments, or even know that others have these sentiments, people who said that they prefer social spending to military spending, who gave that answer on polls, as people overwhelmingly did, assumed that they were the only people with that crazy idea in their heads. They never heard it from anywhere else. Nobody's supposed to think that. Therefore, if you do think it and you answer it in a poll, you just assume that you're sort of weird. Since there's no way to get together with other people who share or reinforce that view and help you articulate it, you feel like an oddity, an oddball. So you just stay on the side and you don't pay any attention to what's going on. You look at something else, like the Superbowl.

To a certain extent, then, that ideal was achieved, but never completely. There are institutions which it has as yet been impossible to destroy. The churches, for example, still exist. A large part of the dissident activity in the United States comes out of the churches, for the simple reason that they're there. So when you go to a European country and give a political talk, it may very likely be in the union hall. Here that won't happen, because unions first of all barely exist, and if they do exist they're not political organizations. But the churches do exist, and therefore you often give a talk in a church. Central American solidarity work mostly grew out of the churches, mainly because they exist.

The bewildered herd never gets properly tamed, so this is a constant battle. In the 1930s they arose again and were put down. In the 1960s there was another wave of dissidence. There was a name for that. It was called by the specialized class "the crisis of democracy." Democracy was regarded as entering into a crisis in the 1960s. The crisis was that large segments of the population were becoming organized and active and trying to participate in the political arena. Here we come back to these two conceptions of democracy. By the dictionary definition, that's an *advance* in democracy. By the prevailing conception that's a *problem*, a crisis that has to be overcome. The population has to be driven back to the apathy, obedience and passivity that is their proper state. We therefore have to do something to overcome the crisis. Efforts were made to achieve that. It hasn't worked. The crisis of democracy is still alive and well, fortunately, but not very effective in changing policy. But it is effective in changing opinion, contrary to what a lot of people believe. Great efforts were made after the 1960s to try to reverse and overcome this malady. One aspect of the malady actually got a technical name. It was called the "Vietnam Syndrome." The Vietnam Syndrome, a term that began to come up around 1970, has actually been defined on occasion. The Reaganite intellectual Norman Podhoretz defined it as "the sickly inhibitions against the use of military force." There were these sickly inhibitions against violence on the part of a large part of the public. People just didn't understand why we should go around torturing people and killing people and carpet bombing them. It's very dangerous for a population to be overcome by these sickly inhibitions, as Goebbels understood, because then there's a limit on foreign adventures. It's necessary, as the *Washington Post* put it rather proudly during the Gulf War hysteria, to instill in people respect for "martial value." That's important. If you want to have a violent society that uses force around the world to achieve the ends of its own domestic elite, it's necessary to have a proper appreciation of the martial virtues and none of these sickly inhibitions about using violence. So that's the Vietnam Syndrome. It's necessary to overcome that one.

It's also necessary to completely falsify history. That's another way to overcome these sickly inhibitions, to make it look as if when we attack and destroy somebody we're really protecting and defending ourselves against major aggressors and monsters and so on. There has been a *huge* effort since the Vietnam war to reconstruct the history of that. Too many people began to understand what was really going on. Including plenty of soldiers and a lot of young people who were involved with the peace movement and others. That was bad. It was necessary to rearrange those bad thoughts and to restore some form of sanity, namely, a recognition that whatever we do is noble and right. If we're bombing South Vietnam, that's because we're defending South Vietnam against somebody, namely, the South Vietnamese, since nobody else was there. It's what the Kennedy intellectuals called defense against "internal aggression" in South Vietnam. That was the phrase used by Adlai Stevenson and others. It was necessary to make that the official and well understood picture. That's worked pretty well.

When you have total control over the media and the educational system and scholarship is conformist, you can get that across. One indication of it was revealed in a study done at the University of Massachusetts on attitudes toward the current Gulf crisis—a study of beliefs and attitudes in television watching. One of the questions asked in that study was, How many Vietnamese casualties would you estimate that there were during the Vietnam war? The average response on the part of Americans today is about 100,000. The official figure is about two million. The actual figure is probably three to four million. The people who conducted the study raised an appropriate question: What would we think about German political culture if, when you asked people today how many Jews died in the Holocaust, they estimated about 300,000? What would that tell us about German political culture? They leave the question unanswered, but you can pursue it. What does it tell us about our culture? It tells us quite a bit. It is necessary to overcome the sickly inhibitions against the use of military force and other democratic deviations. In this particular case it worked. This is true on every topic. Pick the topic you like: the Middle East, international terrorism, Central America, whatever it is—the picture of the world that's presented to the public has only the remotest relation to reality. The truth of the matter is buried under edifice after edifice of lies upon lies. It's all been a marvelous success from the point of view in deterring the threat of democracy, achieved under conditions of freedom, which is extremely interesting. It's not like a totalitarian state, where it's done by force. These achievements are under conditions of freedom. If we want to understand our own society, we'll have to think about these facts. They are important facts, important for those who care about what kind of society they live in.

DISSIDENT CULTURE

Despite all of this, the dissident culture survived. It's grown quite a lot since the 1960s. In the 1960s the dissident culture first of all was extremely slow in developing. There was no protest against the Indochina war until years after the United States had started bombing South Vietnam. When it did grow it was a very narrow dissident movement, mostly students and young people. By the 1970s that had changed considerably. Major popular movements had developed: the environmental movement, the feminist movement, the antinuclear movement, and others. In the 1980s there was an even greater expansion to the solidarity movements, which is something very new and important in the history of at least American, and maybe even world dissidence. These were movements that not only protested but actually involved themselves, often intimately, in the lives of suffering people elsewhere. They learned a great deal from it and had quite a civilizing effect on mainstream America. All of this has made a very large difference. Anyone who has been involved in this kind of activity for many years must be aware of this. I know myself that the kind of talks I give today in the most reactionary parts of the country—central Georgia, rural Kentucky, etc.—are talks of the kind that I couldn't have given at the peak of the peace movement to the most active peace movement audience. Now you can give them anywhere. People may agree or not agree, but at least they understand what you're talking about and there's some sort of common ground that you can pursue.

These are all signs of the civilizing effect, despite all the propaganda, despite all the efforts to control thought and manufacture consent. Nevertheless, people are acquiring an ability and a willingness to think things through. Skepticism about power has grown, and attitudes have changed on many, many issues. It's kind of slow, maybe even glacial, but perceptible and important. Whether it's fast enough to make a significant difference in what happens in the world is another question. Just to take one familiar example of it: The famous gender gap. In the 1960s attitudes of men and women were approximately the same on such matters as the "martial virtues" and the sickly inhibitions against the use of military force. Nobody, neither men nor women, were suffering from those sickly inhibitions in the early 1960s. The responses were the same. Everybody thought that the use of violence to suppress people out there was just right. Over the years it's changed. The sickly inhibitions have increased all across the board. But meanwhile a gap has been growing, and by now it's a very substantial gap. According to polls, it's something like twenty-five percent. What has happened? What has happened is that there is some form of at least semi-organized popular movement that women are involved in—the feminist movement. Organization has its effects. It means that you discover that you're not alone. Others have the same thoughts that you do. You can reinforce your thoughts and learn more about what you think and believe. These are very informal movements, not like a membership organizations, just a mood that involves interactions among people. It has a very noticeable effect. That's the danger of democracy: If organizations can develop, if people are no longer just glued to the tube, you may have all these funny thoughts arising in their heads, like sickly inhibitions against the use of military force. That has to be overcome, but it hasn't been overcome.

PARADE OF ENEMIES

Instead of talking about the last war, let me talk about the next war, because sometimes it's useful to be prepared instead of just reacting. There is a very characteristic development going on in the United States now. It's not the first country in the world that's done this. There are growing domestic social and economic problems, in fact, maybe catastrophes. Nobody in power has any intention of doing anything about them. If you look at the domestic programs of the administrations of the past ten years—I include here the Democratic opposition—there's really no serious proposal about what to do about the severe problems of health, education, homelessness, joblessness, crime, soaring criminal populations, jails, deterioration in the inner cities—the whole raft of problems. You all know about them, and they're all getting worse. Just in the two years that George Bush has been in office three million more children crossed the poverty line, the debt is zooming, educational standards are declining, real wages are now back to the level of about the late 1950s for much of the population, and nobody's doing anything about it. In such circumstances you've got to divert the bewildered herd, because if they start noticing this they may not like it, since they're the ones suffering from it. Just having them watch the Superbowl and the sitcoms may not be enough. You have to whip them up into fear of enemies. In the 1930s Hitler whipped them into fear of the Jews and gypsies. You had to crush them to defend yourselves. We have our ways, too. Over the last ten years, every year or two, some major monster is constructed that we have to defend ourselves against. There used to be one that was always readily available: The Russians. You could always defend yourself against the Russians. But they're losing their attractiveness as an enemy, and it's getting harder and harder to use that one, so some new ones have to be conjured up. In fact, people have quite unfairly criticized George Bush for being unable to express or articulate what's really driving us now. That's very unfair. Prior to about the mid-1980s, when you were asleep you would just play the record: the Russians are coming. But he lost that one and he's got to make up new ones, just like the Reaganite public relations apparatus did in the 1980s. So it was international terrorists and narco-traffickers and crazed Arabs and Saddam

Hussein, the new Hitler, was going to conquer the world. They've got to keep coming up one after another. You frighten the population, terrorize them, intimidate them so that they're too afraid to travel and cower in fear. Then you have a magnificent victory over Grenada, Panama, or some other defenseless third-world army that you can pulverize before you ever bother to look at them—which is just what happened. That gives relief. We were saved at the last minute. That's one of the ways in which you can keep the bewildered herd from paying attention to what's really going on around them, keep them diverted and controlled. The next one that's coming along, most likely, will be Cuba. That's going to require a continuation of the illegal economic warfare, possibly a revival of the extraordinary international terrorism. The most major international terrorism organized yet has been the Kennedy administration's Operation Mongoose, then the things that followed along, against Cuba. There's been nothing remotely comparable to it except perhaps the war against Nicaragua, if you call that terrorism. The World Court classified it as something more like aggression. There's always an ideological offensive that builds up a chimerical

NOAM CHOMSKY

monster, then campaigns to have it crushed. You can't go in if they can fight back. That's much too dangerous. But if you are sure that they will be crushed, maybe we'll knock that one off and heave another sigh of relief.

SELECTIVE PERCEPTION

This has been going on for quite a while. In May 1986, the memoirs of the released Cuban prisoner, Armando Valladares, came out. They quickly became a media sensation. I'll give you a couple of quotes. The media described his revelations as "the definitive account of the vast system of torture and prison by which Castro punishes and obliterates political opposition." It was "an inspiring and unforgettable account" of the "bestial prisons," inhuman torture, [and] record of state violence [under] yet another of this century's mass murderers, who we learn, at last, from this book "has created a new despotism that has institutionalized torture as a mechanism of social control" in "the hell that was the Cuba that [Valladares] lived in." That's the *Washington Post* and *New York Times* in repeated reviews. Castro was described as "a dictatorial goon." His atrocities were revealed in this book so conclusively that "only the most light-headed and cold-blooded Western intellectual will come to the tyrant's defense," said the *Washington Post*. Remember, this is the account of what happened to one man. Let's say it's all true. Let's raise no questions about what happened to the one man who says he was tortured. At a White House ceremony marking Human Rights Day, he was singled out by Ronald Reagan for his courage in enduring the horrors and sadism of this bloody Cuban tyrant. He was then appointed the U.S. representative at the U.N. Human Rights Commission, where he has been able to perform signal services defending the Salvadoran and Guatemalan governments against charges that they conduct atrocities so massive that they make anything he suffered look pretty minor. That's the way things stand.

That was May 1986. It was interesting, and it tells you something about the manufacture of consent. The same month, the surviving members of the Human Rights Group of El Salvador—the leaders had been killed—were arrested and tortured, including Herbert Anaya, who was the director. They were sent to a prison—La Esperanza (hope) Prison. While they were in prison they continued their human rights work. They were lawyers, they continued taking affidavits. There were 432 prisoners in that prison. They got signed affidavits from 430 of them in which they described, under oath, the torture that they had received: electrical torture and other atrocities, including, in one case, torture by a North American U.S. major in uniform, who is described in some detail. This is an unusually explicit and comprehensive testimony, probably unique in its detail about what's going on in a torture chamber. This 160–page report of the prisoners' sworn testimony was sneaked out of prison, along with a videotape which was taken showing people testifying in prison about their torture. It was distributed by the Marin County Interfaith Task Force. *The national press refused to cover it. The TV stations refused to run it.* There was an article in the local Marin County newspaper, the *San Francisco Examiner*, and I think that's all. No one else would touch it. This was a time when there was more than a few "light-headed and cold-blooded Western intellectuals" who were singing the praises of José Napoleón Duarte and of Ronald Reagan. Anaya was not the subject of any tributes. He didn't get on Human Rights Day. He wasn't appointed to anything. He was released in a prisoner exchange and then assassinated, apparently by the U.S.-backed security forces. Very little information about that ever appeared. The media never asked whether exposure of the atrocities—instead of sitting on them and silencing them—might have saved his life.

This tells you something about the way a well-functioning system of consent manufacturing works. In comparison with the revelations of Herbert Anaya in El Salvador, Valladares's memoirs are not even a pea next to the mountain. But you've got your job to do. That takes us toward the next war. I expect, we're going to hear more and more of this, until the next operation takes place.

A few remarks about the last one. Let's turn finally to that. Let me begin with this University of Massachusetts study that I mentioned before. It has some interesting conclusions. In the study people were asked whether they thought that the United States should intervene with force to reverse illegal occupation or serious human rights abuses. By about two to one, people in the United States thought we should. We should use force in the case of illegal occupation of land and *severe* human rights abuses. If the United States was to follow that advice, we would bomb El Salvador, Guatemala, Indonesia, Damascus, Tel Aviv, Capetown, Turkey, Washington, and a whole list of other states. These are all cases of illegal occupation and aggression and severe human rights abuses. If you know the facts about that range of examples, you'll know very well that Saddam Hussein's aggression and atrocities fall well within the range. They're not the most extreme. Why doesn't anybody come to that conclusion? The reason is that nobody knows. In a well-functioning propaganda system, nobody would know what I'm talking about when I list that range of examples. If you bother to look, you find that those examples are quite appropriate.

Take one that was ominously close to being perceived during the Gulf War. In February, right in the middle of the bombing campaign, the government of Lebanon requested Israel to observe U.N. Security Council Resolution 425, which called on it to withdraw immediately and unconditionally from Lebanon. That resolution dates from March 1978. There have since been two subsequent resolutions calling for the immediate and unconditional withdrawal of Israel from Lebanon. Of course it doesn't observe them because the United States backs it in maintaining that occupation. Meanwhile southern Lebanon is terrorized. There are big torture-chambers with horrifying things going on. It's used as a base for attacking other parts of Lebanon. Since 1978, Lebanon was invaded, the city of Beirut was bombed, about 20,000 people were killed, about

80 percent of them civilians, hospitals were destroyed, and more terror, looting, and robbery was inflicted. All fine, the United States backed it. That's just one case. You didn't see anything in the media about it or any discussion about whether Israel and the United States should observe U.N. Security Council Resolution 425 or any of the other resolutions, nor did anyone call for the bombing of Tel Aviv, although by the principles upheld by two-thirds of the population, we should. After all, that's illegal occupation and severe human rights abuses. That's just one case. There are much worse ones. The Indonesian invasion of East Timor knocked off about 200,000 people. They all look minor by that one. That was strongly backed by the United States and is *still* going on with major United States diplomatic and military support. We can go on and on.

That tells you how a well-functioning propaganda system works. People can believe that when we use force against Iraq and Kuwait it's because we really observe the principle that illegal occupation and human rights abuses should be met by force. They don't see what it would mean if those principles were applied to U.S. behavior. That's a success of propaganda of quite a spectacular type.

Let's take a look at another case. If you look closely at the coverage of the war since August (1990), you'll notice that there are a couple of striking voices missing. For example, there is an Iraqi democratic opposition, in fact, a very courageous and quite substantial Iraqi democratic opposition. They, of course, function in exile because they couldn't survive in Iraq. They are in Europe primarily. They are bankers, engineers, architects—people like that. They are articulate, they have voices, and they speak. The previous February, when Saddam Hussein was still George Bush's favorite friend and trading partner, they actually came to Washington, according to Iraqi democratic opposition sources, with a plea for some kind

NOAM CHOMSKY

of support for a demand of theirs calling for a parliamentary democracy in Iraq. They were totally rebuffed, because the United States had no interest in it. There was no reaction to this in the public record.

Since August it became a little harder to ignore their existence. In August we suddenly turned against Saddam Hussein after having favored him for many years. Here was an Iraqi democratic opposition who ought to have some thoughts about the matter. They would be happy to see Saddam Hussein drawn and quartered. He killed their brothers, tortured their sisters, and drove them out of the country. They have been fighting against his tyranny throughout the whole time that Ronald Reagan and George Bush were cherishing him. What about their voices? Take a look at the national media and see how much you can find about the Iraqi democratic opposition from August through March (1991). You can't find a word. It's not that they're inarticulate. They have statements, proposals, calls and demands. If you look at them, you find that they're indistinguishable from those of the American peace movement. They're against Saddam Hussein and they're against the war against Iraq. They don't want their country destroyed. What they want is a peaceful resolution, and they knew perfectly well that it might have been achievable. That's the wrong view and therefore they're out. We don't hear a word about the Iraqi democratic opposition. If you want to find out about them, pick up the German press, or the British press. They don't say much about them, but they're less controlled than we are and they say something.

This is a spectacular achievement of propaganda. First, that the voices of the Iraqi democrats are completely excluded, and second, that nobody notices it. That's interesting, too. It takes a really deeply indoctrinated population not to notice that we're not hearing the voices of the Iraqi democratic opposition and not asking the question, Why? and finding out the obvious answer: because the Iraqi democrats have their own thoughts; they agree with the international peace movement and therefore they're out.

Let's take the question of the reasons for the war. Reasons were offered for the war. The reasons are: aggressors cannot be rewarded and aggression must be reversed by the quick resort to violence; that was the reason for the war. There was basically no other reason advanced. Can that possibly be the reason for the war?

Does the United States uphold those principles, that aggressors cannot be rewarded and that aggression must be reversed by a quick resort to violence? I won't insult your intelligence by running through the facts, but the fact is those arguments could be refuted in two minutes by a literate teenager. However, they never were refuted. Take a look at the media, the liberal commentators and critics, the people who testified in Congress and see whether anybody questioned the assumption that the United States stands up to those principles. Has the United States opposed its own aggression in Panama and insisted on bombing Washington to reverse it? When the South African occupation of Namibia was declared illegal in 1969, did the United States impose sanctions on food and medicine? Did it go to war? Did it bomb Capetown? No, it carried out twenty years of "quiet diplomacy." It wasn't very pretty during those twenty years. In the years of the Reagan-Bush administration alone, about 1.5 million people were killed by South Africa just in the surrounding countries. Forget what was happening in South Africa and Namibia. Somehow that didn't sear our sensitive souls. We continued with "quite diplomacy" and ended up with ample reward for the aggressors. They were given the major port in Namibia and plenty of advantages that took into account their security concerns. Where is this principle that we uphold? Again, it's child's play to demonstrate that those couldn't possibly have been the reasons for going to war, because we don't uphold these principles. But nobody did it—that's what's important. And nobody bothered to point out the conclusion that follows: No reason was given for going to war. None. No reason was given for going to war that could not be refuted by a literate teenager in about two minutes. That again is the hallmark of a totalitarian culture. It ought to frighten us, that we are so deeply totalitarian that we can be driven to war without any reason being given for it and without anybody noticing Lebanon's request or caring. It's a very striking fact.

Right before the bombing started, in mid-January, a major *Washington Post*-ABC poll revealed something interesting. People were asked, If Iraq would agree to withdraw from Kuwait in return for Security Council consideration of the problem of Arab-Israeli conflict, would you be in favor of that? By about two-to-one, the population was in favor of that. So was the whole world, including the Iraqi democratic opposition. So it was reported that two-thirds of the American population were in favor of that. Presumably, the people who were in favor of that thought they were the only ones in the world to think so. Certainly nobody in the press had said that it would be a good idea. The orders from Washington have been, we're supposed to be against "linkage," that is, diplomacy, and therefore everybody goose-stepped on command and everybody was against diplomacy. Try to find commentary in the press—you can find a column by Alex Cock-burn in the *Los Angeles Times*, who argued that it would be a good idea. The people who were answering that question thought, I'm alone, but that's what I think. Suppose they knew that they weren't alone, that other people thought it, like the Iraqi democratic opposition. Suppose that they knew that this was not hypothetical, that in fact Iraq had made exactly such an offer. It had been released by high U.S. officials just eight days earlier. On January 2, these officials had released an Iraqi offer to withdraw totally from Kuwait in return for consideration by the Security Council of the Arab-Israeli conflict and the problem of weapons of mass destruction. The United States had been refusing to negotiate this issue since well before the invasion of Kuwait. Suppose that people had known that the offer was actually on the table and that it was widely supported and that in fact it's exactly the kind of thing that any rational person would do if they were interested in peace, as we do in other cases, in the rare cases that we do want to reverse aggression. Suppose that it had been known. You can make your own guesses, but I would assume that the two-thirds would probably have risen to 98 percent of the population. Here you have the great successes of propaganda. Probably not one person who answered the poll knew any of the things I've just mentioned. The people thought they were alone. Therefore it was possible to proceed with the war policy without opposition.

There was a good deal of discussion about whether sanctions would work. You had the head of the CIA come up and discuss whether sanctions would work. However, there was no discussion of a much more obvious question: Had sanctions already worked? The answer is yes, apparently they had—probably by late August, very likely by late December. It was very hard to think up any other reason for the Iraqi offers of withdrawal, which were authenticated or in some cases released by high U.S. officials, who described them as "serious" and "negotiable." So the real question is: Had sanc-

NOAM CHOMSKY

tions already worked? Was there a way out? Was there a way out in terms quite acceptable to the general population, the world at large and the Iraqi democratic opposition? These questions were not discussed, and it's crucial for a well-functioning propaganda system that they *not* be discussed. That enables the chairman of the Republican National Committee to say that if any Democrat had been in office, Kuwait would not be liberated today. He can say that and no Democrat would get up and say that if I were president it would have been liberated not only today but six months ago, because there were opportunities then that I would have pursued and Kuwait would have been liberated without killing tens of thousands of people and without causing an environmental catastrophe. No Democrat would say that because no Democrat took that position. Henry Gonzalez and Barbara Boxer took that position. But the number of people who took it is so marginal that it's virtually nonexistent. Given the fact that almost no Democratic politician would say that, Clayton Yeutter is free to make his statements.

When Scud missiles hit Israel, nobody in the press applauded. Again, that's an interesting fact about a well-functioning propaganda system. We might ask, why not? After all, Saddam Hussein's arguments were as good as George Bush's arguments. What were they, after all? Let's just take Lebanon. Saddam Hussein says that he can't stand annexation. He can't let Israel annex the Syrian Golan Heights and East Jerusalem, in opposition to the unanimous agreement of the Security Council. He can't stand annexation. He can't stand aggression. Israel has been occupying southern Lebanon since 1978 in violation of Security Council resolutions that it refuses to abide by. In the course of that period it attacked all of Lebanon, still bombs most of Lebanon at will. He can't stand it. He might have read the Amnesty International report on Israeli atrocities in the West Bank. His heart is bleeding. He can't stand it. Sanctions can't work because the United States vetoes them. Negotiations won't work because the United States blocks them. What's left but force? He's been waiting for years. Thirteen years in the case of Lebanon, 20 years in the case of the West Bank. You've heard that argument before. The only difference between that argument and the one you heard is that Saddam Hussein could truly say sanctions and negotiations can't work because the United States blocks them. But

NOAM CHOMSKY

George Bush couldn't say that, because sanctions apparently had worked, and there was every reason to believe that negotiations could work—except that he adamantly refused to pursue them, saying explicitly, there will be no negotiations right through. Did you find anybody in the press who pointed that out? No. It's a triviality. It's something that, again, a literate teenager could figure out in a minute. But nobody pointed it out, no commentator, no editorial writer. That, again, is the sign of a very well-run totalitarian culture. It shows that the manufacture of consent is working.

Last comment about this. We could give many examples, you could make them up as you go along. Take the idea that Saddam Hussein is a monster about to conquer the world—widely believed, in the United States, and not unrealistically. It was drilled into people's heads over and over again: He's about to take everything. We've got to stop him now. How did he get that powerful? This is a small, third-world country without an industrial base. For eight years Iraq had been fighting Iran. That's post-revolutionary Iran, which had decimated its officer corps and most of its military force. Iraq had a little bit of support in that war. It was backed by the Soviet Union, the United States,

Europe, the major Arab countries, and the Arab oil producers. It couldn't defeat Iran. But all of a sudden it's ready to conquer the world. Did you find anybody who pointed that out? The fact of the matter is, this was a third-world country with a peasant army. It is now being conceded that there was a ton of disinformation about the fortifications, the chemical weapons, etc. But did you find anybody who pointed it out? No. You found virtually nobody who pointed it out. That's typical. Notice that this was done one year after exactly the same thing was done with Manuel Noriega. Manuel Noriega is a minor thug by comparison with George Bush's friend Saddam Hussein or George Bush's other friends in Beijing or George Bush himself, for that matter. In comparison with them, Manuel Noriega is a pretty minor thug. Bad, but not a world-class thug of the kind we like. He was turned into a creature larger than life. He was going to destroy us, leading the narco-traffickers. We had to quickly move in and smash him, killing a couple hundred or maybe thousand people, restoring to power the tiny, maybe eight percent white oligarchy, and putting U.S. military officers in control at every level of the political system. We had to do all those things

NOAM CHOMSKY

because, after all, we had to save ourselves or we were going to be destroyed by this monster. One year later the same thing was done by Saddam Hussein. Did anybody point it out? Did anybody point out what had happened or why? You'll have to look pretty hard for that.

Notice that this is not all that different from what the Creel Commission when it turned a pacifistic population into raving hysterics who wanted to destroy everything German to save ourselves from Huns who were tearing the arms off Belgian babies. The techniques are maybe more sophisticated, with television and lots of money going into it, but it's pretty traditional.

I think the issue, to come back to my original comment, is not simply disinformation and the Gulf crisis. The issue is much broader. It's whether we want to live in a free society or whether we want to live under what amounts to a form of self-imposed totalitarianism, with the bewildered herd marginalized, directed elsewhere, terrified, screaming patriotic slogans, fearing for their lives and admiring with awe the leader who saved them from destruction, while the educated masses goosestep on command and repeat the slogans they're supposed to repeat and the society deteriorates at home. We end up serving as a mercenary enforcer state, hoping that others are going to pay us to smash up the world. Those are the choices. That's the choice that you have to face. The answer to those questions is very much in the hands of people like *you* and *me.*

NOAM CHOMSKY